Fathers of the Church on Mary

Marco Pappalardo

WITH MARIAN PRAYERS AND REFLECTIONS

Libreria Editrice Vaticana

United States Conference of Catholic Bishops
Washington, DC

English translation copyright © 2012, Libreria Editrice Vaticana. All rights reserved.

Cover image © Philippe Lissac/Godong/Corbis

First printing, March 2012

ISBN 978-1-60137-149-2

CONTENTS

Introduction vii

Meditations. 1

Marian Prayers and Reflections. 35

Acknowledgments. 56

Index of Church Fathers 59

For my mother

INTRODUCTION

Just as the divine Maternity is the means through which Mary has an absolutely unique relationship with Christ and is present in the work of human salvation accomplished by Christ, so also it is above all from the divine Maternity that the relationships between Mary and the Church flow. This is because Mary is the Mother of Christ, who, as soon as he took on human nature in her virginal womb, united to himself as Head his mystical Body, the Church. So Mary, as Mother of Christ, is also to be held to be the Mother of all the faithful and pastors, meaning the Church.[1]

After the publication of my previous books *Advent and Christmas with the Church Fathers* and *Lent and Easter with the Church Fathers*, I now intend simply to make known the thoughts of some Fathers of the Church on Mary, the Mother of Jesus. These will be thirty-one Marian reflections for a monthly meditation on the Holy Virgin. The writings of the Fathers are among the most important documents of the Church's tradition in terms of the richness of their contents on different levels: spiritual, moral, dogmatic, and ascetic.

In March of 2007, the Holy Father Benedict XVI began a series of presentations on the Fathers of the Church in the Wednesday general audiences. The previous series had been dedicated to the Apostles. They are part of an ongoing, profound catechesis to present the Church through the life of men who were great figures of the first centuries of Christianity. Each time, the attention is focused on highlighting the originality and relevance of each Father, often known to few, so that instead they may be brought within reach of all.

This book, in the masterful footsteps of the Holy Father, is intended to get the Fathers out of the libraries or the patristic anthologies in order to present them to all, including to those who are not specialists, scholars, or enthusiasts. It is not a text for study, but is intended to be an instrument of accompaniment for personal and group meditation.

Those who wish to learn more about these extraordinary figures can seek out works of great value, extensive and rich collections, monumental volumes, and monographic texts, which are now easier and easier to find.

Every passage of this book is accompanied by an introduction written by the author, to set the stage for the contents and bring them up to date.

Marco Pappalardo

Note

1   Pope Paul VI, Speech at the conclusion of the third session of Vatican Council II, (Libreria Editrice Vaticana: Vatican City, 1964).

Meditations

John Damascene, *Homily on the Dormition of Mary*, 1, 14

Let's begin these reflections with a prayer to the Blessed Mother, that she may accompany us on the paths of life. Let us offer to her our hearts, needs, desires, dreams, burdens, pains, and joys of every day, certain that she will lead us to Christ, she who is the Mother of hope.

We, too, turn to you today, Lady, Virgin and Mother of God, binding our souls to your hope as to the most solid and sure anchor. To you we consecrate our minds, souls, bodies, our whole selves, honoring you with psalms, hymns, and spiritual songs as we are able, since we will never be able to perform such a task as it truly deserves. . . . But you, Good Lady, Mother of the Good Lord, help us and steer our destinies wherever you wish; quell the violence of our base passions and guide us, once the storm has been calmed, into the tranquil harbor of the divine will, considering us worthy of the beatitude to come, of that kindly light that radiates from the vision of the Word of God who took flesh from you. To him, together with the Father and the most holy and good and life-giving Spirit, be glory, honor, power, majesty, and magnificence, now and ever and unto the ages of ages! Amen.

Augustine, *Tractates on the Gospel of St. John,* 10, 3

It is not recommendations and contacts that matter in the Gospel, not even ancestry! It is not enough to go to Mass every Sunday to set our consciences at ease, nor is making pilgrimages and processions of all kinds enough to obtain a place in heaven! In the Our Father, we ask that his will and not ours be done, not as defenseless and submissive persons, but as beloved and blessed children. Mary, who was a mother, certainly kept in her heart the fact that she was a daughter loved by God in a special way, obedient to his will and to his Word.

When Jesus, who was talking with his disciples, was told that his mother and brothers were outside, he said: *Who is my mother, and who are my brothers? And, stretching out his hand toward his disciples, he said: Here are my brothers, because whoever does the will of my Father who is in heaven is my brother, my sister, and my mother.* So that means Mary, too, because she did the will of the Father. This is what God praised in her—not so much the fact that she had generated the flesh of his Son from her flesh as the fact that she did the will of the Father.

Balaj the Syrian, *Prayers and Hymns*, 3, 6

The Old Testament is full of figures, images, and prophecies in which the Magisterium, the Fathers of the Church, its doctors and saints all, recognize the proclamation of her who gave to the world the awaited Messiah. From Genesis to the book of the prophet Isaiah—passing through the historical and wisdom books and then to the last prophets—prefigurations and other proclamations relative to the Virgin Mother of the Savior run through all the texts of the Old Testament.

Blessed are you, Mary, because in you the enigmas and mysteries announced by the prophets have found their solution. Moses depicted you in the burning bush and in the cloud, Jacob in the ladder, David in the ark of the covenant, and Ezekiel in the closed and sealed door. And behold, in your giving birth today all of those mysteries have been fulfilled. Praise to the Father who has sent his only-begotten Son, born of Mary, freeing us from error and glorifying her memory on earth and in heaven. Blessed are you, Mary, who have conceived him. Blessed you who have given birth to him. Blessed you who have nourished him who nourishes all. Blessed you who have borne in your womb the Mighty One, who in his power bears the world and governs all. . . . Blessed are you, because with your milk you nourished God, who in his mercy has become small in order that the wretched may become great.

Ephrem the Syrian, *Hymn for the Birth of Christ*, 1

Mary's "yes" is the special measure of all our "yeses" to the Lord. Her adherence to God's plan becomes a model for our participation in the divine plan in this world. Mary was "the daughter of her son," and we will be regenerated in his mercy as children if we live our daily lives in praise of the Most High and in service to our brothers and sisters.

Turn your eyes to Mary! When Gabriel came to her and began to speak with her, she asked, "How can this be?" And the servant of the Holy Spirit replied to her, saying, "It is easy for God, because for him all is possible." And she, believing firmly in what she had heard, said, "Behold the handmaid of the Lord." And immediately the Word descended, hovered over her, entered and inhabited her without her noticing anything. And so she conceived him without suffering anything; and he became a child in her womb, while the whole world was full of him. . . . So when you hear about the birth of God, remain in silence: let Gabriel's words be imprinted on your spirit! Nothing is too difficult for that supreme majesty who lowered himself to be born among us and from us.

James of Batna, *Hymn to the Most Holy Virgin*

There are no words that suffice when speaking of the Blessed Mother; we can only fumble blindly in an effort to get a little closer. This does not mean that Mary is far away and distant from her children; on the contrary, she is close as a woman, mother, and disciple who accepted with courage and humility the great gift of the Holy Spirit. The attitude of those who look to her must be the attitude of those who are searching for their mother's home, a filial devotion that must shape the heart of each one by its gentle discipline.

O Son of the Virgin, permit me to speak of your Mother; for all I know, she is a topic too lofty for us! . . . How could I paint this wonderful portrait with ordinary colors, if even the most exquisite palette is insufficient? Her beauty is too lofty, too stupendous for my colors, and I do not dare even to hope that my spirit could represent it adequately. It is easier to depict the splendor and blaze of the sun than to express the magnificence of Mary in words. It is perhaps possible to represent in colors a splendid wheel of fire, but no speech is sufficient to proclaim Mary fully. . . . Who could ever be able to praise her enough?

Augustine, *Tractates on the Gospel of St. John, 10, 3*

Mary is the model of obedience to the will of God and knows well what it means to base one's life on the plan of God in history. It is a history of abandonment that also applies to us and is renewed moment by moment when we focus everything on love for him and for our neighbor. Mary teaches us humble adherence to the Word of Jesus, which is worth more than anything else.

While the crowd was full of admiration for the Lord, seeing the miracles and wonders that manifested what was hidden in his flesh, someone shouted, in the grip of enthusiasm: *Blessed the womb that bore you.* And Jesus: *Blessed, rather, are those who listen to the Word of God, and observe it.* As if to say: Even my mother, whom you have called blessed, is blessed because she observes the Word of God, not because the Word was made flesh in her and dwelt among us; because she kept the Word of God by means of which she was created and who was made flesh in her. Let human beings not enjoy children according to the flesh; let them rather exult if they are united with God in their spirits.

Ephrem the Syrian, *Hymn for the Birth of Christ*, 1

The artists have depicted her in the most varied ways, the poets have called her by countless epithets, the litanies could be infinite. Let us always remember that looking at Mary means looking at Jesus, speaking of Mary means speaking of Jesus, praying to Mary means praying to Jesus. No mother would look away from her son in his suffering or in his triumph, and so through her we reach Jesus.

Today Mary is a heaven for us, because she bears God. The most high divinity, in fact, lowered himself and took up habitation in her; in her, he became small so that we might be great; in her, he took on a garment for us, so that redemption might take place for us. In Mary, the sayings of the prophets and of the just were fulfilled. From her the light arose for us, and the darkness of paganism disappeared. She has many names, and it is a joy for me to call her by them. She is the rock in which the mighty King of kings dwells. . . . She is also a new heaven, because the King of kings dwells in her. He entered into her and then he came out, dressed in the appearance of the external world. . . . She is the spring from which living water comes for the thirsty; those who have tasted this drink bear fruit a hundredfold.

Rabbula of Edessa, Liturgical Hymns, 1-5

Mary is above all Mother and continues her mission as Mother of the Church. To her, the humble servant in whom the Lord has done great things, we entrust ourselves in order to become witnesses of the inexhaustible love of her Son. Yes, with Mary we must be ready to anticipate and fight against all the evils that threaten life, the dignity of the person, the poor, the small, the weak, the abandoned, the sick in body and spirit, and creation, that endanger the happiness and even the salvation for which we must strive.

Hail Mary, all-holy Mother of God, marvelous and splendid treasure of the whole world, radiant light, dwelling of the Incomprehensible, pure temple of the Creator of all things! Hail, because through you was announced to us the one who took away the sins of the world and redeemed it. How will we praise you, O Humble One, you who are all holy, you who grant all the faithful help and strength? All of us in this world look up and await hope and salvation from you, O Humble One. Strengthen our faith and give peace to the whole world. For this we faithful praise you as the throne of the cherubim and as the dwelling of God in time. Pray and implore him for all of us, so that our souls may be saved from the wrath to come.

Augustine, *Tractates on the Gospel of St. John, 8, 9*

Bishop Sigalini of Palestrina writes in regard to the passage of the Gospel about the wedding of Cana: "I don't know if, when two young people get married, they are concerned about inviting the Blessed Mother to the wedding. She was at Cana and resolved every difficulty, she acted as a godmother, so to speak, for this decision of love. In this way she began a presence that would be, and still is, guaranteed in the life of every Christian." Mary was always present in the fundamental moments of the life of Jesus; and so let us, with prayer and devotion, call upon her on the journey of our life.

Why, therefore (at the wedding of Cana), did the Son say to the mother: "What have I to do with you, woman? My hour has not yet come"? Our Lord Jesus Christ was God and man; as God, he did not have a mother; as man, he did. She was therefore the mother of his flesh, the mother of his humanity, the mother of the infirmity that he made his own for our sake. . . . With that response, therefore, the Lord intends to distinguish, in the faith of believers, who he is and how he came. He came by means of a woman, who is his mother, he who is God and Lord of heaven and earth. . . . He is, at the same time, Mary's Lord and Mary's Son. Do not be amazed that he is, at the same time, Son and Lord: he is called Son of Mary as he is also called Son of David, and he is Son of David because he is Son of Mary.

Cyril of Alexandria, *Against Those Who Do Not Acknowledge Mary as the Mother of God*, 4

"The daughter of Adam, Mary, consenting to the word of God, became the Mother of Jesus. Committing herself whole-heartedly to God's saving will and impeded by no sin, she devoted herself totally, as a handmaid of the Lord, to the person and work of her Son, under and with him, serving the mystery of redemption, by the grace of Almighty God" (*Lumen Gentium*, no. 56). With the title of "Mother of God," the Church emphasizes the mission of Mary in salvation history, a mission that lies at the foundation of the devotion of the Christian people. Let us walk in faith with Mary, "Mother of the Church," and with the Church, "our mother."

The Word himself, becoming incarnate in the Blessed Virgin, made her flesh his temple: the one who came forth was, from the external point of view, man, but on the inside, true God. . . . He, for his part, being truly God, destined for himself, at the moment of clothing himself with humanity, in the fullness of time, a manner of being born different from that of anyone else. She who is rightly considered blessed must therefore be called "Mother of God" and "Virgin Mother": he was not just any sort of man, in fact, that Jesus who was born from her.

Rabbula of Edessa, *Liturgical Hymns*, 1-5

The Blessed Mother intercedes with Jesus for us, and he certainly grants the prayers of his Mother and gives us what we truly need according to God's plan. We often do not know what to ask for, or, on the contrary, we prefer to use too many words. We entrust to Mary what our heart desires but does not dare to ask for, what our tongue is not able to express, the thoughts of our mind, because she is able to interpret these like a mother who understands the needs of a child who is not yet able to speak.

O Mother most pure, help us who are poor, as you are wont to do. You see how we, children of the earth, approach our end and become lost. Implore the gift of grace for us by your intercession, O pure and holy Virgin. Plead for us continually, that our wickedness may not bring us to ruin, and turn to us, O blessed one, as you pray to your only-begotten, the Son who came forth from you, that he may have mercy on us through your holy prayer. Hail, O ship that brings new life to humanity. Hail, O holy rock to which the King of kings descended to live there. Hail, O humble Virgin, Mother of God. Take on our behalf to your only-begotten, to the Son who came forth from you, all of our supplications, so that he may have mercy on us through your holy prayer.

Balaj the Syrian, *Prayers and Hymns*, 3, 6

There is a close relationship between Mary and peace, because the Mother of Jesus welcomed into her heart God, true peace, inner peace. She teaches the way of peace with oneself and with others at the moment in which we welcome God into our hearts. It is only in this way that our view of reality can change and our decisions, our actions, our words, can become makers of peace in the name of Jesus.

Glory to you, O our refuge! Glory to you, O our boast, because through you our race has been raised up to heaven. Beseech God, who was born from you, to send peace and calm upon his Church. By the power of your prayers, O Mother of the Most High, may he give the world and its inhabitants the fullness of peace! Praise to him who came from Mary, who made her his mother and became a child in her. Blessed be the King of kings who has become man and raised up the human race to the heights of heaven. Praise to the one who sent him for our redemption, and glory to the Holy Spirit who takes away our sins!

James of Batna, *Hymn to the Most Holy Virgin*

"The Father of mercies willed that the incarnation should be preceded by assent on the part of the predestined mother, so that just as a woman had a share in bringing about death, so also a woman should contribute to life. . . . Hence not a few of the early Fathers freely assert . . . in their preaching: 'the knot of Eve's disobedience was untied by Mary's obedience: what the virgin Eve bound through her disbelief, Mary loosened by her faith.' Comparing Mary with Eve, they call her 'Mother of the living,' and frequently claim: 'death through Eve, life through Mary'" (*Lumen Gentium*, no. 56).

She is blessed among women, through whose work the curse was removed from the earth and the chastisement came to an end. She is the pure one, the humble one, radiant with the brilliance of all holiness, of whom my mouth is truly insufficient to speak. She is the poor one who became the mother of the King and gave abundance to the thirsty world to bring it life. She is the ship that brought us the treasures and goods of the Father's house and poured out its riches upon our desolate land. She is the good field that, without seed, bore abundant crops, and without being cultivated, produced a rich harvest. She is the second Eve who among the mortal gave birth to Life, loosening and eliminating the debt of her mother. She is the daughter who reached out her hand to her downtrodden foremother and lifted her out of the chasm into which the serpent had hurled her.

John Damascene, *Homily on the Dormition of Mary*, 1, 10-11, 12-13

The apocryphal Gospels recount that Mary was taken up into heaven by Jesus himself in the presence of the Apostles, of some women, and of the angels. The Blessed Mother experienced in their fullness all the most important events of the life of Jesus, sharing his mission and holiness. Jesus himself, taking her with him to the Father, crowned her as Queen of Heaven and Co-redemptrix by virtue of the merits that come from the Cross and Resurrection.

The body of her who, in spite of giving birth, preserved her virginity, was preserved, despite death, in such a way as not to be corrupted, but on the contrary to be changed into an even more grandiose and divine tabernacle, immune to death and destined to endure unto the ages of ages. . . . We therefore do not call your sacred dormition "death," but rather "sleep" or "voyage," or, to put it better, "arrival." . . . Your soul, in fact, did not descend among the dead, and your flesh did not see corruption. Your body, immaculate and exempt from any contamination, was not left upon the earth, but you, O Queen, lady and mistress, true Mother of God, you were assumed into the royal heavenly dwelling. Heaven drew to itself her whose greatness was superior to that of heaven.

Paulinus of Nola, *Carme 6*, 111-131

"Rejoice" is the greeting of the angel Gabriel to Mary. Let us also rejoice in the memory of such an event, let us rejoice in encountering Jesus in the Eucharist. Blessed is Mary for having done the will of God, and blessed are we for all of the times when, at the school of the Virgin, we are able to say our "yes" with faith even in suffering and in difficult situations.

O maiden, the angel said to her, more blessed than all the virgins who ever were, are, and will be in all the universe that the circle of the sun encompasses, chosen by the great God to be called mother of him whose Father he himself is! Happily you conceive a son, without ever having had relations with any man, pure of all human contact, made fecund by the Word of God. Your womb gives a body to him who created the heavens, the earth, the sea, the stars, who always was and is now and will ever be the Lord of the world and Creator of light. And he, the Light of Heaven, through you will clothe himself with mortal members and present himself to the eye and to the multitude of humanity. Raise up your tranquil thoughts to a gift of glory so great; you will receive strength from him who wished to be your son, although he is Son of God.

James of Batna, *Hymn to the Most Holy Virgin*

Like Mary, let us love the precepts of Jesus and put them into practice within ourselves and in our daily activities, so that between faith and life there may be not distance, but consistency and synthesis. Beatitude is attained by doing the will of God in truth, with humility, for love. The Blessed Mother opens to us the gates of heaven; let us open the doors of our hearts!

Behold, henceforth all generations shall call me blessed," Mary said in the illumination of her soul, thinking of her Son. She saw to what lofty heights she had been elevated, she saw that the world would glorify her with the highest admiration. She could already see the future and proclaimed that the people would proclaim her virginity blessed. She had learned from the Holy Spirit that her Son would reign over all peoples; therefore she claimed from all tongues their tribute of praise and honor. For this we too blessedly praise this blessed one, whose blessedness itself is too high for the tongues of the whole world. . . . She is blessed because she bore, embraced, and clasped to her heart as her own Son that eternal hero who upholds the world with his hidden power.

Justin, *Dialogue with Trypho*, 100

In spite of our weakness, God always remains faithful to his covenant of love. In his mysterious plan, he renews humanity with visible signs of mercy. Mary, Virgin and Mother of God, is at the same time instrument and protagonist of the action of divine grace, trusting the proclamation of the Angel. We too are called to be new men and women, secure in faith, strong in testimony, firm in hope.

We also know that he became man by means of the Virgin, so that the disobedience originated by the serpent might be eliminated the same way it had begun. Eve, a virgin without fear, conceived the word of the serpent and gave birth to disobedience and death; Mary, the Virgin, conceived faith and joy at hearing from the angel Gabriel the good news that the Spirit of the Lord would come upon her and the power of the Most High would overshadow her, wherefore the holy being to be born from her would be Son of God; and she replied: *Let it be done to me according to your word.* Thus from her was generated him to whom we have demonstrated that so many Scriptures refer, through whom God destroys the serpent as also the angels and human beings who have become like him, and frees from death those who repent of their errors and believe in him.

James of Batna, *Hymn to the Most Holy Virgin*

What a splendid encounter, that of Mary and the angel Gabriel! What heavenly words we too hear from the Gospel! The angel was sent to your home, O Blessed Virgin, and since then all go to you, they invoke you, they love you, great and small, rich and poor, from every part of the world. We too come to you, saying, "Turn to us your eyes of mercy," the same eyes that you turned to the messenger from God, the same eyes with which you looked at Jesus in the crib and beneath the Cross, the eyes of the Resurrection, of peace between heaven and earth.

It was a wonderful moment, when Mary spoke with Gabriel. The humble daughter of poverty and the angel engaged in an astonishing conversation. The pure Virgin and the luminous angel held a dialogue that restored peace between heaven and earth. One out of all the women from here below concluded with the prince of the angelic hosts an accord on the reconciliation of the whole world. They were like judges sitting down to reconcile the realities of heaven with those of earth: they spoke, listened, and established peace between the contending parties. The Virgin and the angel came together and brought everything back into order. . . . The great saga that began under the tree came to a conclusion and was completely resolved, so much so that the result was peace. Heaven and earth spoke together as friends. . . . Gabriel rebuilt the edifice knocked down by the serpent; Mary rebuilt the house demolished by Eve in paradise.

Ambrose, *Commentary on the Gospel of St. Luke*, II, 16

Mary is a woman of humble and attentive listening, of the ears and above all of the heart, a fecund listening preserved with care, a listening in order to understand and share, patient and humble. A woman of silence and at the same time of essential, powerful, decisive words, given out of love. She always listened to the voice of God who spoke to her in situations, in persons, in what happened to her. She listened to the words of Jesus—what a marvelous gift! Mary's listening continues for all of us!

Finally, *Behold*, she said, *the handmaid of the Lord: be it done to me according to your word*. See what humility, see what dedication! She calls herself handmaid of the Lord who has been chosen as his mother, nor does she exalt herself at the unexpected promise. In calling herself handmaid, she did not claim any privilege from such tremendous grace, willing to do what was commanded of her. Called to give birth to him who is meek and humble, she too had to be a model of humility. You have the proof of deference, you see her desire. *Behold the handmaid of the Lord*—this is the demonstration of her willingness for anything; *let it be done to me according to your word*—this is the expression of her desire.

John Damascene, *Second Homily on the Dormition of Mary*, 10-11

We read from *Munificentissimus Deus*, the apostolic constitution with which Pope Pius XII, on November 1, 1950, defined the dogma of the Assumption of Mary: "For which reason, after we have poured forth prayers of supplication again and again to God, and have invoked the light of the Spirit of Truth, for the glory of Almighty God who has lavished his special affection upon the Virgin Mary, for the honor of her Son, the immortal King of the Ages and the Victor over sin and death, for the increase of the glory of that same august Mother, and for the joy and exultation of the entire Church; by the authority of our Lord Jesus Christ, of the Blessed Apostles Peter and Paul, and by our own authority, we pronounce, declare, and define it to be a divinely revealed dogma: that the Immaculate Mother of God, the ever Virgin Mary, having completed the course of her earthly life, was assumed body and soul into heavenly glory."

The King comes to his own Mother, taking into the divine and unblemished hands her soul, pure and immaculate. She must have addressed him, then, in words like these: "Into your hands, my son, I entrust my spirit. Accept my soul, which is dear to you, which you preserved without stain. To you, not to the earth, I deliver my body: keep it unharmed, since it pleased you to dwell there and in being born you preserved its virginity. Take me to you, so that where you are, the fruit of my womb, I too may dwell with you." . . . And what happens? The elements, I suppose, move and change; one hears mighty voices and sounds, hymns of the angels who precede, accompany, follow, some escorting the immaculate and most holy soul, ascending with her who ascends to heaven, until they have brought the queen to the royal throne, the others surrounding the divine and sacred body and singing to the Mother of God such hymns as suit the angels.

James of Batna, *Hymn to the Most Holy Virgin*

Marian devotion must not be something passive, but militant, made of entrustment, belonging, availability, service. It is not the dimension of "doing things," whether visible or not, but of becoming models and credible witnesses of the love of God; it is therefore life itself that is speaking in this way, singing the Magnificat in the everyday.

H e looked at her humility, her kindness, and her purity, and he dwelt in her, because he willingly shares his presence with the humble, as he himself says: *To whom shall I ever attend, if not to the meek and the humble?* He saw that she was the most humble of the children of men, and because of this he dwelt in her, as she herself attests: that is, that he looked upon her humility and dwelt in her. Therefore we must praise her, since she is so pleasing to God. . . . In fact, the Lord, who glorifies according to the measure of humiliation, has raised her up to become his mother. What could ever compare to her humility?

Anonymous, *Homily on the Assumption of the Blessed Virgin Mary*

Who knows how intensely Mary looked at her little Jesus; who knows how moving were the kisses, the caresses, and the embraces of Mary for her little Jesus; who knows how sweet for Mary were his crying and his laughter. We know, however, that one day we will enjoy all of this in the presence of God!

O happy Mary! O glorious Mother! O sublime birth-giver, to whom the maker of heaven and earth entrusts himself! O happy kisses planted by the lips of the suckling child! Already aware in his infancy, he, recognizing that he was your Son, played with you, his Mother; while as true Son of the Father, he commanded you as Lord. You conceived and brought to light, poor in time, your Maker, who was your Creator before time began. O happy birth, praised by saints, necessary for the lost, salutary for the victors! You are blessed and glorious, O Virgin Mary, in all of this, for all of this you are worthy of praise, you who have merited the gift of fecundity while not losing the privilege of virginity. Blessed are you among women, you are chosen among all the ranks of virgins, you will follow the Lamb wherever he goes.

Origen, *Homilies on the Song of Songs*, II, 6

Being in the shadow of God means being under his protection, cradled, cuddled, made strong! Like Mary, we can find refuge under the wings of the Most High, and, looking to her, our hearts can become a welcoming manger, so that Jesus may be born in us and through us may be given to the world. But there's more! Our Lady, the glorious and blessed Virgin, covers us with her mantle, and beneath her protection we can find shelter.

I t is said that *the Holy Spirit will come upon you, and the power of the Most High will overshadow you.* The birth of Christ therefore had its origin in a shadow; and it is not only in Mary that his birth began with a shadow, but also in you, if you are worthy, that the Word of God is born. So act in such a way as to be able to receive his shadow, and when you have become worthy of the shadow, his Body, so to speak, will come to you, from which the shadow is born: since *those who are faithful in little things will be so in great things as well.*

John Damascene, *Second Homily on the Dormition of Mary*, 18-19

Some artistic representations show us the Blessed Mother holding the child Jesus, not huddled up against her, but stretched out and offered to humanity. It is the image of Mary Help of Christians, who offers Jesus to the world and the world to Jesus. Each of us can imagine being Jesus in the arms of Mary. She cares for us the same way she did for him!

It was necessary that the Mother of God should enter into possession of the goods of the Son, and as Mother of God and handmaid should be honored by all creation. The inheritance of the parents usually passes to the children: but in this case, to use the words of a wise man, "the sacred streams return to their source." The Son has subjected all of creation to his Mother. . . . Let us therefore make our memory the treasury of the Mother of God. In what way? If we carefully avoid our former vices and sincerely love the virtues, seeking to have them as companions, she will frequently visit her servants, bringing with her the entourage of all good things; she will bring with her Christ her Son, King and Lord of the Universe, who will dwell in our hearts.

Cyril of Alexandria, *Homily 4*, no. 1183

The Fathers of the Church have in common their speaking of Mary, Mother of God, with a linguistic register that is sublime but at the same time capable of making us feel close to her. There is such poetry in them, but they are verses that bring us beside her as if she were near. Their words seem to come from heaven, because only the language of the angels can say of the Blessed Mother what we can only babble.

Hail, Mother of God, Mary, venerable treasure of the whole world, inextinguishable lamp, crown of virginity, scepter of sound doctrine, indestructible temple, house of him who cannot be contained in any house, Mother and Virgin; through whom the Gospels call blessed him who comes in the name of the Lord: hail, you welcomed into your holy and virginal womb the immense and uncontainable, through you the Holy Trinity is glorified and worshiped; through you the precious Cross is celebrated and adored all over the world; through you the heavens exult, through you the angels and archangels rejoice, through you the demons are put to flight, through you the tempter Devil falls from heaven, through you the degraded creature is brought to heaven. . . . And who could ever adequately celebrate Mary, most worthy of all praise? She is Mother and Virgin; O marvelous thing! This miracle fills us with amazement.

Cosmas the Singer, *Carme*, 1899

The saints have a special devotion for the Blessed Mother, and their thoughts express this abundantly, like this one from the Holy Curé of Ars: "The Most Holy Virgin acts as mediatrix between her Son and us. In spite of the fact that we are sinners, she is full of tenderness and compassion for us. Is not the son who has cost his mother the most tears perhaps the one closest to her heart? Does not the mother always take the most care, perhaps, of the weakest and most defenseless?" Let us follow the way of the saints, let us enroll in the school of Mary, let us love Jesus in the sacraments, in the Word, in the Church, in our neighbor.

Blessed Mother of God, open to us the door of your benevolence. Do not disappoint the trust of us who hope in you; free us from our adversities. You are the salvation of the human race. The number of my sins is so great, O Mother of God! I run to you, O Immaculate, in search of salvation. Console my desolate soul and ask your Son, our God, to grant me the forgiveness of my sins, O Immaculate One, only blessed one! I place all of my hope in you, O Mother of the Light; welcome me under your protection.

Ambrose, *On Virgins*, II, 2, 12-13

Mary teaches us wisdom, concreteness, service, the ability to wait, hope, courage, humility, trust, charity. Our hearts are receptacles that preserve all of these gifts and many others, disclosed to us under the Cross that was their key. We are called to reflect on modesty, on sobriety, and above all on meditative and fecund silence, and to make concrete decisions in a society of noise, of rumor, of gossip, of empty words.

No sooner did Mary know that she had been chosen by God than she became even more humble and immediately set out for the mountains to visit her cousin; and not, of course, because her faith needed confirmation, since she had already consented to the divine message. In fact, she heard it said: *Blessed is she who has believed!* And she stayed with her for three months. Over such a long span of time, she was not seeking proofs for her faith, but giving proof of her charity. And all of this after the child, rejoicing in his mother's womb, had greeted the Mother of the Lord. . . . When all of those wonders then followed—a sterile woman giving birth, the fecundity of a virgin, the words of a mute, the adoration of the Magi, the anticipation of Simeon, the witness of the star—Mary, who although she troubled at the entrance of the Angel was imperturbable before so many miracles, *stored up*, as is written, *all of these things in her heart.*

John Damascene, *The Orthodox Faith*, 3, 12

"We can ask ourselves: Why, among all woman, did God choose Mary of Nazareth? The answer is hidden in the unfathomable mystery of the divine will. Nonetheless, there is one reason that the Gospel highlights: her humility. This is emphasized well by Dante Alighieri in his last Canto of the Paradiso: 'Virgin Mary, daughter of your Son, / more humble and exalted than any other creature, / the fixed end of eternal counsel . . .' Yes, God was attracted by the humility of Mary, who found grace in his eyes (cf. Lk 1:30). She thus became the Mother of God, image and model of the Church, chosen among the peoples to receive the blessing of the Lord and to spread it to the whole human family. This 'blessing' is nothing other than Jesus Christ himself" (Pope Benedict XVI, *Angelus*, December 8, 2006).

We proclaim, in an absolute sense, that the Holy Virgin is properly and truly Mother of God. Just as, in fact, it is God who was born from her, so also, as a result, she is Mother of God who generated the true God who took flesh from her. We say that God, without a doubt, was born from her, not because the divinity took the principle of existence from her, but because the Word himself, who was generated before the ages, beyond all time, in the last times enclosed himself within her womb for our salvation. . . . The Holy Virgin, in fact, did not generate a mere man, but the true God. . . . Rightly and truly, therefore, we call Mary the Holy Mother of God. This name, in fact, contains the whole mystery of the Incarnation.

Ambrose, *On Virgins*, II, 2, 7

Mary, the Mother of Jesus, is present in all the fundamental moments of the life of her Son and of the emerging Church. She does not say many words, but each of them has tremendous weight for the economy of salvation. St. Ambrose tells about Mary in everyday life, speaking of her with the wisdom that comes from on high, showing her as a sublime model of virtue, but accessible to each one of us. In praying the Rosary, perhaps we should add in one of these attributes of the Blessed Mother every now and then, so that the prayer may be fruitful in our lives, and not remain mere words.

Now, what is nobler than the Mother of God? What is more splendid than she who generated the Body of Christ without contaminating her own? And truly, what remains to be said of the other virtues? She was virgin not only in body, but also in soul, because she never stained the transparency of her spirit with any ambiguous aspiration: she was humble of heart, austere in speech, prudent in soul, measured in her words, but very eager to learn; she placed her hope not in the unsure possession of riches, but in the prayers of the poor; diligent in work, discreet in hearing conversations, she wanted as the sole judge of her soul not man, but God; she never contradicted anyone, loved everyone, moved aside for the elderly, fled from vainglory, followed good sense, loved virtue.

Ephrem, *Carme* 18, 1

"Hail, star of the sea / glorious mother of God / ever-Virgin Mary / happy gate of heaven. The 'Ave' of the heavenly host / brings the proclamation of God, / changes the fate of Eve / brings peace to the world. Break the chains of the oppressed, / bring light to the blind, / drive away all evil, / obtain for us all good. / Show yourself as Mother of all, / offer up our prayer, / may Christ receive it kindly, / he who became your Son. / Virgin holy among all others, / gentle queen of heaven, / make your children innocent, / humble and pure of heart. / Give us days of peace, / watch over our path, / bring us to see your Son, / full of joy in heaven. / Praise to the Father most high, / glory to Christ the Lord, / may the hymn of faith and love go up / to the Holy Spirit. Amen." Let us make it our habit and cause of joy to praise Mary Immaculate with hymns, songs, and prayers.

Eve became guilty of sin, and the debt was passed to Mary, so that the daughter might pay the debts of the mother and tear up the sentence that had handed down its tears to all generations. Mary carried the fire in her hands and cradled the flame in her arms; she gave her breasts to the flame, and gave milk to him who nourishes all things. Who is able to speak of her? . . . Mary is the clearest spring, without any conjugal influence: she welcomed into her womb the river of life, which irrigated the world with its waters and brought life to all the dead. . . . Two mothers have appeared who have generated different children: one generated a man who cursed her, and Mary generated God, who fills the world with blessing.

John Damascene, *Homily on the Dormition of Mary*, 3, 5

We began this journey of reflection on the Blessed Mother through the Fathers of the Church with a prayer of entrustment to the Mother of God; let us conclude our journey with another prayer, an invocation as children who want to live in the grace of God on earth, in order to be worthy citizens of heaven. Let us pray to Mary, we are in her hands!

Accept the good will that transcends our capacities, give us salvation, free us from the vices of the soul, heal the evils of the body, defeat the adversaries, allow us to lead a tranquil life and give us the light of the Spirit. Kindle in us the love of your Son, and make our lives pleasing to him. Grant that, after becoming participants in your beatitude, seeing the glory of your Son shine in you, we may sing sacred hymns in eternal joy, together with those who worthily celebrate the solemnity of the Spirit, in honor of him who, through you, worked our salvation, Christ, Son of God and our God, to whom be glory and power together with the Father and the most holy and life-giving Spirit, now and ever and unto the ages of ages. Amen.

Marian Prayers and Reflections

Alma Redemptoris Mater

The Alma Redemptoris Mater, which dates from the eleventh century, is one of the four antiphons sung after Night Prayer. It is used in the Advent Season.

L oving mother of the Redeemer,
gate of heaven, star of the sea,
assist your people who have fallen yet strive to rise
again.
To the wonderment of nature you bore your Creator,
yet remained a virgin after as before.
You who received Gabriel's joyful greeting,
have pity on us poor sinners.

Alma Redemptoris Mater, quae pervia caeli
porta manes, et stella maris, succurre cadenti,
surgere qui curat, populo: tu quae genuisti,
natura mirante, tuum sanctum Genitorem,
Virgo prius ac posterius, Gabrielis ab ore
summens illud Ave, peccatorum miserere.

Ave Regina Caelorum

The Ave Regina Caelorum is one of the four antiphons sung after Night Prayer. It is used in Lent.

Hail, Queen of heaven;
Hail, Mistress of the Angels;
Hail, root of Jesse;
Hail, the gate through which the Light rose over the earth.
Rejoice, Virgin most renowned and of unsurpassed beauty.

Ave, Regina caelorum,
ave, Domina angelorum,
salve, radix, salve, porta,
ex qua mundo lux est orta.
Guade, Virgo gloriosa,
super omnes speciosa;
vale, o valde decora,
et pro nobis Christum exora.

Regina Caeli

The Regina Caeli is a twelfth-century antiphon for Evening Prayer during the Easter Season. Since the thirteenth century, it has been used as the seasonal antiphon in honor of the Blessed Virgin after Night Prayer.

Queen of heaven, rejoice, alleluia.
The Son whom you merited to bear, alleluia,
has risen as he said, alleluia.
Pray for us to God, alleluia.
Rejoice and be glad, O Virgin Mary, alleluia!
For the Lord has truly risen, alleluia.

Let us pray;
O God, who through the resurrection of your Son, our
Lord Jesus Christ, did vouchsafe to give joy to the world;
grant, we beseech you, that through his Mother, the Virgin
Mary, we may obtain the joys of everlasting life.
Through the same Christ our Lord.
Amen.

Regina caeli, laetare, alleluia:
quia quem meruisti portare, alleluia.
Resurrexit, sicut dixit, alleluia.
Ora pro nobis Deum, alleluia.
Gaude et laetare, Virgo Maria, alleluia.
Quia surrexit Dominus vere, alleluia.

Oremus.
Deus, qui per resurrectionem Filii tui Domini nostri
Iesu Christi mundum laetificare dignatus es, praesta,
quaesumus, ut per eius Genetricem Virginem Mariam
perpetuae capamus gaudia vitae.
Per Christum Dominum nostrum.
Amen.

Salve, Regina

The Salve, Regina is one of four Marian antiphons sung at the end of Night Prayer, according to the season. It was possibly written by Hermann the Lame, a monk of Reichenau (1013-1054), or by Adhemar, bishop of Le Puy (d. 1098). The Salve, Regina was also used as a processional antiphon at the Abbey of Cluny (France) from around 1135.

Hail, Holy Queen, Mother of Mercy,
our life, our sweetness and our hope.
To thee do we cry,
poor banished children of Eve.
To thee do we send up our sighs,
mourning and weeping in this valley of tears.
Turn then, most gracious advocate,
thine eyes of mercy toward us,
and after this our exile
show unto us the blessed fruit of thy womb, Jesus.
O clement, O loving,
O sweet Virgin Mary.

Salve, Regina,
mater misericordiae;
vita, dulcedo et spes nostra, salve.
Ad te clamamus,
exsules filii Evae.
Ad te suspiramus gementes et flentes
in hac lacrimarum valle.

Eia ergo, advocate nostra,
Illos tuos misericordes oculos ad nos converte.
Et Iesum benedictum fructum ventris tui,
nobis, post hoc exsilium, ostende.
O Clemens, o pia, o dulcis Virgo Maria.

Memorare

The Memorare is a sixteenth-century version of a fifteenth-century prayer that began "Ad sanctitatis tuae pedes, dulcissima Virgo Maria." Claude Bernard (1588-1641) popularized the idea that the Memorare was written by St. Bernard.

Remember, O most gracious Virgin Mary, that never was it known that anyone who fled to thy protection, implored thy help, or sought thy intercession, was left unaided. Inspired by this confidence, I fly unto thee, O Virgin of virgins, my Mother. To thee do I come, before thee I stand, sinful and sorrowful. O Mother of the Word Incarnate, despise not my petitions, but in thy mercy hear and answer me. Amen.

Memorare, o piissima Virgo Maria, non esse auditum a saeculo, quemquam ad tua currentem praesidia, tua implorantem auxilia, tua petentem suffragia, esse derelictum. Ego tali animatus confidentia, ad te, Virgo Virginum, Mater, curro, ad te venio, coram te gemens peccator assisto. Noli, Mater Verbi, verba mea despicere; sed audi propitia et exaudi. Amen.

Sub tuum praesidium

This prayer, known in Latin as "Sub tuum praesidium" and first found in a Greek papyrus, c. 300, is the oldest known prayer to the Virgin.

We fly to thy protection, O holy Mother of God.
Despise not our petitions in our necessities,
but deliver us always from all dangers
O glorious and blessed Virgin.

Sub tuum praesidium confugimus,
sancta Dei Genetrix;
nostras deprecationes ne despicias
in necessitatibus;
sed a periculis cunctis libera nos semper,
Virgo gloriosa et benedicta.

Sancta Maria, succurre miseris

Holy Mary, succor the miserable, help the faint-hearted, comfort the sorrowful, pray for thy people, plead for the clergy, intercede for all women consecrated to God; may all who keep thy holy commemoration feel now thy help and protection.

A Prayer from the Maronite Liturgy

The following prayer is taken from "Ramsho," or Evening Prayer, (Common of the Blessed Virgin Mary) from the Prayer of the Faithful or Divine Office of the Syriac Maronite Antiochene Church.

Father,
author of all goodness,
we adore you who gave Mary the grace of innocence
from the time of her conception.
O Son and Word eternal,
we exalt you who appeared in time for our salvation as
the Son of Mary.
O Holy Spirit, glory be to you who chose Mary as
your spouse,
for by you all generations proclaim her blessed.

O God,
Through her intercession keep us from all harm
and let us always do good by keeping your commandments
and by pleasing you.
With her we will praise you for ever.
Amen.

Angelus Domini

The custom of saying the Hail Mary three times at the ringing of the bell in the evening goes back to the thirteenth century. Bells from that period were often inscribed with the angelic salutation. Today, it is the custom to say the "Angelus" three times: in the morning, at noon, and in the evening. The closing prayer was formerly the post-Communion for Masses of our Lady in Advent and is now the opening prayer for the Fourth Sunday of Advent.

V/. The Angel of the Lord declared unto Mary.
R/. And she conceived of the Holy Spirit.
Hail Mary . . .

V/. Behold the handmaid of the Lord.
R/. Be it done unto me according to thy word.
Hail Mary . . .

V/. And the Word was made flesh.
R/. And dwelt among us.
Hail Mary . . .

V/. Pray for us, O Holy Mother of God,
R/. That we may be made worthy of the promises of Christ.

Let us pray;
Pour forth, we beseech thee, O Lord, thy grace into our hearts; that we, to whom the Incarnation of Christ, thy Son, was made known by the message of an angel, may by his Passion and Cross be brought to the glory of his Resurrection. Through the same Christ our Lord. Amen.

A Hymn of Praise to Mary from the Byzantine Liturgy

This hymn of praise known as the "Megalynarion" (or "Great Hymn to the Theotokos") is taken from the Divine Liturgy of St. John Chrysostom of the Byzantine Rite. "Theotokos" (Greek for "God-bearer" or Mother of God) is Mary's most ancient title.

It is proper to call you blessed,
ever-esteemed Theotokos, most pure, and mother of
God.
You who are more worthy of honor than the cherubim
and far more glorious than the seraphim.
You who incorruptibly gave birth to God the Word,
verily Theotokos, we fervently extol you.

Maria, Mater gratiae

Mary, Mother of grace and Mother of mercy, shield me from the enemy and receive me at the hour of my death.

Singing the Praises of Mary

You are raised higher than the Cherubim,
you are extolled above the Seraphim,
because you have drawn down your Son,
and have carried him in your arms,
and nursed him with your milk!
If I say that you are heaven,
behold you are worthy of honor
more than the heavens of heaven,
because he who is above the Cherubim
has come and has taken flesh from you
without harming your virginity!
Blessed are you O Mary! Queen,
O immaculate lamb, O Mother of the King!
Your name will be blessed in all times
by the mouths of the faithful, who will shout out saying:
Hail Mary! To you a holy "Ave"!
Hail to her who is worthy of honor
more than all the earth!
Hail Mary! A holy "Ave"!
Hail to the Virgin of all sorrows!
Hail Mary! A holy "Ave"!
Hail to the Queen, to her who is the daughter of the King!
Hail Mary! A holy "Ave"!
Hail to the new heaven that is now on earth!
Hail Mary! A holy "Ave"!
Hail to her of whose greatness the patriarchs were proud!
Hail Mary! A holy "Ave"!
Hail to her whose honor the prophets foretold!

Indeed, we beg you, O Mary, O queen,
intercede for us with Christ the King.
And you, O Lord, through the intercession of the Mother
of God, Holy Mary,
give us the grace of the forgiveness of our sins.

Akathist Hymn

Hail Mary! Hail, the restoration of the fallen Adam!
Hail, the redemption of the tears of Eve.
Intercede for us with the Lord.

Hail Mary! Height, hard to climb, for human minds;
Hail, depth, hard to explore, even for the eyes of
angels.
Intercede for us with the Lord.

Hail Mary! Throne of wisdom;
Hail, security and hope for all who call upon you.
Intercede for us with the Lord.

Hail Mary! Heavenly ladder by which God came down
to earth;
Hail, bridge leading from earth to heaven.
Intercede for us with the Lord.

Hail Mary! Favor of God to mortals;
Hail, Mary, access of mortals to God.
Intercede for us with the Lord.

Hail Mary! Mother of the Lamb and of the Good
Shepherd;
Hail, fold for the sheep of his pasture.
Intercede for us with the Lord.

Hail Mary! Never silent voice of the apostles;
    Hail, never conquered courage of champions.
Intercede for us with the Lord.

Hail Mary! Mother of the Star which never sets;
    Hail, dawn of the mystic day.
Intercede for us with the Lord.

Litany of the Blessed Virgin Mary (Litany of Loreto)

The Litany of Loreto, a Marian litany, contains invocations that date back to the twelfth century. It was recorded in its present form (apart from a few additions by recent popes) at Loreto in 1558 and approved by Sixtus V (1521-1590). For about half of the invocations, the present translation uses the traditional renderings, which have been in use since the seventeenth century.

Lord, have mercy	Lord, have mercy
Christ, have mercy	Christ, have mercy
Lord, have mercy	Lord, have mercy
God our Father in heaven	have mercy on us
God the Son, Redeemer of the world	have mercy on us
God the Holy Spirit	have mercy on us
Holy Trinity, one God	have mercy on us
Holy Mary	pray for us
Holy Mother of God	pray for us
Most honored of virgins	pray for us
Mother of Christ	pray for us
Mother of the Church	pray for us
Mother of divine grace	pray for us
Mother most pure	pray for us
Mother of chaste love	pray for us
Mother and virgin	pray for us
Sinless Mother	pray for us
Dearest of mothers	pray for us
Model of motherhood	pray for us
Mother of good counsel	pray for us
Mother of our Creator	pray for us
Mother of our Savior	pray for us

Virgin most wise	pray for us
Virgin rightly praised	pray for us
Virgin rightly renowned	pray for us
Virgin most powerful	pray for us
Virgin gentle in mercy	pray for us
Faithful Virgin	pray for us
Mirror of justice	pray for us
Throne of wisdom	pray for us
Cause of our joy	pray for us
Shrine of the Spirit	pray for us
Glory of Israel	pray for us
Vessel of selfless devotion	pray for us
Mystical Rose	pray for us
Tower of David	pray for us
Tower of ivory	pray for us
House of gold	pray for us
Ark of the covenant	pray for us
Gate of heaven	pray for us
Morning Star	pray for us
Health of the sick	pray for us
Refuge of sinners	pray for us
Comfort of the troubled	pray for us
Help of Christians	pray for us
Queen of angels	pray for us
Queen of patriarchs and prophets	pray for us
Queen of apostles and martyrs	pray for us
Queen of confessors and virgins	pray for us
Queen of all saints	pray for us
Queen conceived without sin	pray for us
Queen assumed into heaven	pray for us

Queen of the rosary	pray for us
Queen of families	pray for us
Queen of peace	pray for us
Lamb of God, you take away the sins of the world	have mercy on us
Lamb of God, you take away the sins of the world	have mercy on us
Lamb of God, you take away the sins of the world	have mercy on us

Pray for us, holy Mother of God. That we may become worthy of the promises of Christ.

Let us pray.
Eternal God, let your people enjoy constant health in mind and body. Through the intercession of the Virgin Mary free us from the sorrows of this life and lead us to happiness in the life to come. Grant this through Christ our Lord. Amen.

From a Sermon by St. Sophronius, Bishop

(Oratio 2, in Sanctissimae Deiparae Annuntiatione, 21-22. 26: PG 87, 3, 3242. 3250)

Through Mary the Father's blessing has shone forth on mankind

Hail, *full of grace, the Lord is with you.* What joy could surpass this, O Virgin Mother? What grace can excel that which God has granted to you alone? What could be imagined more dazzling or more delightful? Before the miracle we witness in you, all else pales; all else is inferior when compared with the grace you have been given. All else, even what is most desirable, must take second place and enjoy a lesser importance.

The Lord is with you. Who would dare challenge you? You are God's mother; who would not immediately defer to you and be glad to accord you a greater primacy and honor? For this reason, when I look upon the privilege you have above all creatures, I extol you with the highest praise: *Hail, full of grace, the Lord is with you.* On your account joy has not only graced men, but is also granted to the powers of heaven.

Truly, *you are blessed among women.* For you have changed Eve's curse into a blessing; and Adam, who hitherto lay under a curse, has been blessed because of you.

Truly you are blessed among women. Through you the Father's blessing has shone forth on mankind, setting them free of their ancient curse.

Truly, you are blessed among women, because through you your forebears have found salvation. For you were to give birth to the Savior who was to win them salvation.

Truly, you are blessed among women, for without seed you have borne, as your fruit, him who bestows blessings on the whole world and redeems it from that curse that made it sprout thorns.

Truly, you are blessed among women, because, though a woman by nature, you will become, in reality, God's mother. If he whom you are to bear is truly God made flesh, then rightly do we call you God's mother. For you have truly given birth to God.

Enclosed within your womb is God himself. He makes his abode in you and comes forth from you like a bridegroom, winning joy for all and bestowing God's light on all.

You, O Virgin, are like a clear and shining sky, in which God *has set his tent*. From you *he comes forth like a bridegroom leaving his chamber*. Like a giant running his course, he will run the course of his life which will bring salvation for all who will ever live, and extending from the highest heavens to the end of them, it will fill all things with divine warmth and with life-giving brightness.

Acknowledgments

Scripture excerpts used in this work are taken from the *New American Bible, revised edition* © 2010, 1991, 1986, 1970 Confraternity of Christian Doctrine, Inc., Washington, DC. All rights reserved. No part of this work may be reproduced or transmitted in any form or by any means, electronic or mechanical, including photocopying, recording, or by any information storage and retrieval system, without permission in writing from the copyright owner.

Excerpts from *Vatican Council II: The Conciliar and Post Conciliar Documents* edited by Austin Flannery, OP, copyright © 1975, Costello Publishing Company, Inc., Northport, NY, are used with permission of the publisher, all rights reserved. No part of these excerpts may be reproduced, stored in a retrieval system, or transmitted in any form or by any means—electronic, mechanical, photocopying, recording, or otherwise—without express written permission of Costello Publishing Company.

Excerpts from *Manual of Indulgences*, copyright © 2006, Libreria Editrice Vaticana–United States Conference of Catholic Bishops, Washington, DC. All rights reserved.

Excerpts from *The Liturgy of the Hours* © 1974, International Commission on English in the Liturgy Corporation. All rights reserved.

The "Akathist Hymn" is taken from *Mother of God*
© 1982 by Lawrence Cunningham, Scala Books
(HarperCollins) and is used with permission.

Permission to use other passages cited in this book was
graciously provided by the publishers, to whom we
express our thanks. Excerpts were translated directly from
the Italian edition of this book:

Bosio, G., E. Dal Covolo, and M. Maritano. *Introduzione
ai Padri della Chiesa: Secoli III e IV* [Introduction to the
Church Fathers: Third and Fourth Centuries]. Turin, Italy:
SEI, 1993.

Bosio, G., E. Dal Covolo, and M. Maritano. *Introduzione
ai Padri della Chiesa—Secoli IV e V* [Introduction to the
Church Fathers: Fourth and Fifth Centuries]. Turin, Italy:
SEI, 1995.M. Starowieyski, J. Miazek (eds.), *I Padri vivi*,
Città Nuova, Rome 1982

La teologia dei padri: Volume 2 [The Theology of the
Fathers: Volume 2]. Rome, Italy: Città Nuova, 1974.

Pellegrino, M. *Vox Patrum*. Turin, Italy. SEI, 1963.

Origen. *Omelie sul Cantico dei Cantici*. M.I. Danieli (ed.).
Città Nuova, Rome, 1990.

About the Author

Marco Pappalardo is a Salesian Cooperator, a past member of the National Council for Youth Pastoral Care of the Italian Bishops' Conference, and a member of the diocesan office for social communications of the Archdiocese of Catania, in Italy. He is a freelance journalist and author of several books in Italian. He is a literature teacher at Don Bosco High School in Catania.

Index of Church Fathers

Ambrose
Commentary on the Gospel of St. Luke
II, 16   20

On Virgins
II, 2, 12-13   29
II, 2, 7   31

Anonymous
*Homily on the Assumption of the
    Blessed Virgin Mary*   24

Augustine
Tractates on the Gospel of St. John
10, 3   3, 7
8, 9   10

Balaj the Syrian
Prayers and Hymns
3, 6   4, 13

Cosmas the Singer
Carme, 1899   28

Cyril of Alexandria
Against Those Who Do Not Acknowledge
*   Mary as the Mother of God*
4   11

Homily 4
no. 1183   27

Ephrem
Carme
18, 1   32

Ephrem the Syrian
Hymn for the Birth of Christ
1   5, 8

James of Batna
Hymn to the Most Holy Virgin   6, 14,
                                    17, 19, 23

John Damascene
Homily on the Dormition of Mary
1, 14   2
3, 5   33
1, 10-11, 12-13   15

Second Homily on the Dormition of Mary
10-11   21
18-19   26

The Orthodox Faith
3, 12   30

Justin
Dialogue with Trypho
100   18

Origen
Homilies on the Song of Songs
II, 6   25

Paulinus of Nola
Carme 6
111-131   16

Rabbula of Edessa
Liturgical Hymns
1-5   9, 12